This book belongs to

_____

This book is dedicated to my children - Mikey, Kobe, and Jojo.

Wright Brothers

By Mary Nhin

Illustrated By
Yuliia Zolotova

I'm Wilbur and this is my younger brother, Orville.
We were keen inventors, even as children.

Our passion started one day when our father came home with a gift. He tossed it in the air. Instead of falling to the floor, as we expected, it flew across the room until it struck the ceiling, where it fluttered awhile, and finally sank to the floor. When it broke, we built ourselves a new one from sticks and rubber bands. It was our first flying machine!

Neither of us finished high school because we moved around too often to keep up with our studies, but we became skilled mechanics from our hobbies. We made a living repairing bicycles, motors, and other machinery. We even designed and built our own mechanical printing press, but we were most fascinated by dreams of flying.

Our work with bicycles, in particular, influenced our belief that an unstable vehicle such as a flying machine could be controlled and balanced with practice.

We had seen great minds try and fail to pilot flying machines, and we resolved to build upon their work by designing a flying machine of our own.

Our father supported us, but he made us promise that we could never fly together. He was scared of losing both his sons if there was ever an accident.

We started with kites and gliders, using the experiments and calculations of scientists such as Chanute and Lilienthal.

But our initial machines were disappointing. I test piloted the glider we had built, but I couldn't gain nearly as much height as we'd expected, and I had a terrible time controlling the thing.

Our wing design couldn't give us enough lift. And the steering was unpredictable, sometimes even doing exactly the opposite of what I was telling it to do!

I was disappointed and complained to my brother that we might not ever be successful.

We were saddened, but we were also stubborn, so we kept trying. We failed so many times and went back to the drawing board every time to work out what had caused our glider to perform so badly. Flying was our passion, and we were not about to give up.

We conducted many experiments and eventually designed a new aircraft, that was powered by a real engine, like a car. Finally, one day, our design was a success. We had created the world's very first airplane.

We had achieved what we thought was impossible, all because we had kept trying.

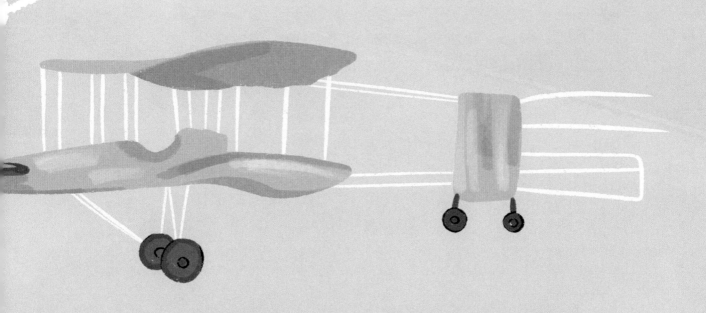

If we worked on the assumption that what is accepted as true really is true, then there would be little hope for advance.

Timeline

1902 - Wrights create controllable aircrafts

1903 - Wrights make four short flights with
         powered airplane

1909 - Wilbur and Orville receive the
         Congressional Medal of Honor

1910 - The brothers receive the Langley
         Medal from President Howard Taft

1930 - The Wright brothers are awarded the
         Daniel Guggenheim Medal

1962 - The brothers become two of the first men
         to be inducted into the Aviation Hall of Fame

minimovers.tv

 @marynhin   @GrowGrit
#minimoversandshakers

 Mary Nhin   Ninja Life Hacks

 Ninja Life Hacks

 @marynhin

Made in the USA
Las Vegas, NV
10 June 2023

73251460R00024